Sawdust to Satisfaction: Stress-free Remodeling

The Book on Choosing the Right General Contractor Every Time!

By Michael A. Baum

Baum Construction & Development
(562)-42-4BAUM (2286)
www.BaumCon.com

Sawdust to Satisfaction: Stress-free Remodeling
The Book on Choosing the Right General Contractor Every Time!

Copyright © Michael Baum 2014

Foreword

Years ago the world was more trusting; a handshake was all it took to have someone's word, and the contractor's reputation always preceded him.

But these days, our cities are bigger, there are many more contractors to choose from, and reputation doesn't always get around. We move around more and need to find contractors quickly. Thus, fly-by-night operators abound, out to scam the unsuspecting, ready to make a quick buck and then disappear.

It is unfortunate that so many of these unprofessional contractors leave a bad taste in the mouths of homeowners, when so many good contractors are in the business of doing a good job. Contractors like Michael Baum. In his impressive 40 years in the business, he has listened to the wishes of homeowners and made it happen. That is why he has earned the Angie's list Super Service Award for the last four years. A contractor like him is in it for the long haul, and will make sure his reputation stays rock solid.

These days, consumers must be savvy. They must do their research. They must ask questions and observe. Michael walks you through how to do each of the steps. Consumers must also protect themselves, Michael covers ways to reduce your liability when remodeling. The information contained in this book will be invaluable to anyone planning to do any remodeling project. Michael has condensed 40 years of experience working with clients into a "how to" book for homeowners.

This is a comprehensive "must read" if you are planning a remodeling project. That is why I am glad to see this book in print. What Michael Baum explains is what every homeowner needs to know.

Once homeowners do find that quality contractor, be it through word of mouth, Angie's List or other resource, by utilizing the information contained in this book they are sure to develop a relationship that will last for years to come.

Raymond Aaron
New York Times Best Selling Author / Real Estate Investor / Educator / Speaker

Table of Contents

Introduction

California—it is a beautiful place to live and a place where dreams are made. As a licensed general contractor in the greater Long Beach area, I've helped many homeowners' dreams come true. From new home construction to remodeling a home, it is rewarding working with homeowners to make their home work for them. A home unique to a homeowner is truly a dream come true.

General Contractor Michael Baum with former California governor Arnold Schwarzenegger.

As I have grown my business over 40 years, it has been important to me to offer integrity in my work. This, I believe, is key to helping homeowners achieve their dreams.

Unfortunately, I've also seen many homeowners' dreams turn into nightmares. When people choose the wrong contractor, things can go terribly wrong. What I sometimes see is the aftermath of that bad choice.

These homeowners then call me to fix things. It's hard to watch as they try to get over the headache and wasted money from paying the wrong contractor to do their home renovations. With some key knowledge in the area, these homeowners could have avoided these issues.

That is why I wrote this book. I want to help those looking to find a trusted general contractor, whether building a new home or renovating an existing home, to have their dreams met right the first time. There are many things to look for when starting your home remodeling journey, and I can help. I invite you to take the time to read my book so you can find the best contractor to take care of your home.

I suggest that you read this book twice, once before you select your contractor, and once during your project to make sure it is proceeding the way you've planned.

Chapter 1
Construction Basics

Congratulations! You are either thinking about a home construction project, or actually planning one. Doing a project will either excite you, or fill you with dread...maybe even both.

I think the reason for all of this emotion is twofold: your home is typically the largest single investment of your lifetime, and it's also the structure that protects your family and gives you a place to raise your children. How could a decision to change that not be filled with emotion?

While there can be many sub-areas to construction, the main ones are:

•**New construction**. This is when a new building is started from scratch. This has many advantages because the work does not have to be done within the parameters of an existing structure.

•**Remodeling**. This, on the other hand, is the exact opposite. You have existing space, walls and structure that have to be incorporated into the project. There are also existing "hidden" items such as electrical, duct work, etc., that must be taken into account.

•**Addition/Remodel**. This is a blend of both types of construction from above. The addition portion is new construction but it has to be blended with the existing structure. The remodel portions are as I described above.

Why Remodel?
Remodeling your home is a huge undertaking, and it can be done for a number of different reasons. Some people want to improve the resale value of their home by adding upgrades, while others want to improve the usability and utility of their home. Others remodel their home to make room for a growing family, or because they are fulfilling their dreams.

The reality is that most remodeling is done for a specific occasion. It could be a wedding, a graduation, maybe friends are coming to visit and you want to spruce up the kitchen, or perhaps you might be expecting an addition to the family and you need more space.

Regardless of the reason you're considering a remodel to your home, you'll find that it can be a very complex process—from determining if you need a building permit to ensuring that your remodel meets current building code requirements and much more.

Why Hire a Contractor?

Going it alone is not a particularly good idea. There is a lot that can go wrong, there are a lot of schedules and items to consider, and you may not realize the magnitude of what you are undertaking. Working with a trusted general contractor is usually the best solution. However, not all general contractors are created equal, and you'll need to know how to choose the right professional, and how to work with your contractor throughout the process.

This book will help you understand why you should hire a contractor, as well as what qualities to look for in a reputable general contractor, and how to maintain a professional, friendly relationship throughout the process.

It goes deeper than that, too – this book also lists the items that homeowners should consider when choosing a contractor, as well as the top remodeling options to give you the highest return on your investment.

Chapter 2
Do It Yourself vs Hiring a Contractor

Open almost any home magazine or watch any show on a home network, and you'll find a number of ugly "before" pictures and stunning "after" pictures. Read the article or watch the show, and you'll come away thinking, "Wow, that looks so easy!"

With the number of do-it-yourself TV shows out there, and how simple some people can make remodeling look, you might be tempted to go it alone when planning to remodel your home. As a general contractor in the business for 40 years—please follow my advice and don't be fooled. There is a reason these projects look easy.

Remodel Show vs Reality

I live in California, near the epicenter of many TV shows. Once, a television show invited me to bid a kitchen remodel for their program. I met with the producers and discussed the scope of work. I asked some basic questions: what was their budget, and what was the timeline to complete the project?

Experience told me that the work that they were asking to be done, including labor and materials, was valued at around $25,000 and would take three weeks to complete in order to do quality work. Their response left me in shock.

They told me that they had a *$12,000 budget* and the project needed to be done in just *nine days.*

When I declined to bid they said, "We have a really difficult time getting contractors to do our work because of the small budgets and the short timelines. In order to complete the show, we have to bring in set carpenters from the studio to get the job done."

What people see is not even close to reality. What they see is made to look "easy." When viewers see home remodeling on TV, they are not aware of what to expect in the real world, and they get a totally unrealistic view of the costs and the timelines to do remodeling projects.

That results in "sticker shock" when they go into the real world and get pricing for their project from real contractors. In some cases, it can also cause clients to think that contractors are trying to take advantage of them.

So then some homeowners figure they can do their own remodeling projects to save money. While doing things on your own is fine with relatively simple projects (such as repainting the family room, for instance), however, many jobs are complex and require experience, skill and specialized tools to be completed correctly.

Time vs Money

Unfortunately, some homeowners look only at the amount of money that might "save" doing it themselves, and not at the amount of time and effort that is going to be expended on their part. Jobs that a contractor might complete in weeks might take a homeowner months to complete; there can be added costs to starting and stopping the remodel, working on it during nights and weekends; all of this on top of working a full-time job.

In addition, as a homeowner you might find that your state requires the remodel job be done by a professional with a contractor's license. Jobs that require building permits, and those that are over a certain dollar amount in terms of labor and material, are usually the domain of licensed professionals. This is important to know before starting a project, yet many homeowners don't do their homework.

Besides that, there are numerous other reasons to hire a licensed contractor to handle your remodeling project. For example, the right contractor will be insured in case something untoward happens during the job; also, the right contractor will be able to obtain building permits for the job, and he or she will probably know the local building inspector and what to expect. The right contractor will have also undergone a background check from the state in order to obtain a license, which offers significant peace of mind.

Recently in California, officials conducted a sting operation to catch unlicensed contractors. The fraud team posed as homeowners wanting bids on remodel projects; what they found were many swindlers who not only were acting as contractors looking to make money dishonestly, but several also had criminal histories, some of them violent criminal histories. In all, 12 unlicensed contractors were arrested.

Besides protecting yourself and your family from potential hazards, other benefits include:

- A quality contractor will hire reputable subcontractors.
- A quality contractor will ensure that all jobs are done to code.
- By using a quality contractor you avoid costly mistakes, repairs, and delays.
- You will save money in the long run with a quality general contractor.

Notice I say, a "quality contractor" on each benefit; this is because not all contractors are created equal. Not only should you check that your contractor is reputable, you should also make sure you choose one that specializes in the type of project that you are proposing.

Homeowner as General Contractor

I've had many clients attempt to be their own general contractor, typically in an effort to save money. Most times, they end up hiring me or another contractor to complete the job.

When they first start a project, they think, "It's not that is that difficult, not rocket science," but they don't have the years of experience needed to make that assessment.

Trying to act as your own general contractor and work at your full-time job is very difficult. Once part-way in, it's much easier to see why remodeling work should be managed by a professional contractor.

The key mistake that I see time and time again is the homeowner gets the first contractor in and gets the work started, and then waits until that work is complete before looking for the next contractor. This is usually because they are unfamiliar with the process, what comes first and what follows. This results in delays at almost every trade.

As a professional, when I start the job, I have a schedule already put together and my subcontractors lined up to arrive at the appropriate times. I also have connections with subcontractors I know will do quality work and do the work on time. This saves the homeowner time and money in the long run.

Not only that, I know building codes; when I open up a wall, I know what to look for and if something needs fixing. And if down the road you want to sell your house, you'll be glad you hired a quality contractor, as you will need to disclose the type of work done, and whether it was done by a licensed professional.

Chapter 3
Type of Project

As I mentioned, not all contractors are created equal. This has nothing to do with whether they are good, competent contractors. Contractors tend to specialize in specific areas of construction. Some focus on brand-new ground-up construction, some specialize in kitchens, others in bathrooms, and still others may specialize in room additions. While all general contractors can do all of these types of work, you will want to talk to ones who are doing your type of project.

The caveat here is that projects tend to run in trends. For instance, in my business, I will have a period where I'm doing kitchens or bathrooms, and then it will switch to room additions, and then possibly whole house remodels. See what types of projects that contractors you interview are doing at the present time.

Do your homework. Collect photographs of the types of things that you might want to have done in your project go to model homes and take photographs, write down what you want to have included in your project. Be very detailed. Write down everything that you want, versus what you can afford. You may be surprised at how much of your wish list you can actually get for your budget. Pick out your materials ahead of time. For instance, if you would like to have a plug or switch in a specific location, write it down.

Design/Architect Plans
When I go out on an initial consultation, more times than not I advise the clients to engage an architect or designer. It is important to have their vision captured on paper for each contractor to bid.

Later on, I'll talk about getting "apples for apples" bids. Having plans to bid from alleviates most of this problem. I do have one caveat about construction plans, not all plans are 100% complete. There is almost always something to be worked out on site. This is very common and typically not a big deal.

Costs & Bids

It is a rare occasion when potential clients are not surprised by the real world costs. It is almost always more expensive than the consumer thinks it's going to be.

It was out of this persistent conversation that I adopted my spreadsheet bid. Presenting a bid to a potential client with no reference as to how the costs were arrived at was very frustrating for them. That's why I show them all the costs associated with the job. They may not like the final number, but at least they know how it all adds up.

While we're talking about costs, let's talk about the budget. No matter the amount of your budget, you should "plan" to have an additional 25% for additional expenditures during the project. During the course of construction, when walls are open, it is the least expensive time to make upgrades or additions.

Typically, once the demolition is done, clients can "see" possibilities that they had never considered before. For instance, maybe they want to add on framing for a skylight, a door, or a future window; or perhaps they suddenly want to add in plumbing for a future bathroom, or maybe even get everything in place for a future room addition. It is a very rare job that the clients don't wish to add something along the way; and added changes mean added costs.

Many of the costs can be controlled by the client. The amenity level that you choose directly and sometimes dramatically impacts the budget. I've had clients that are perfectly okay with a $200 toilet and others that chose a $2,000 toilet. Tile is another area that can impact the budget very quickly. We've installed tile all that costs $5 per square foot, and other tile that costs

$65 per square foot. A reputable contractor can and will assist you with choosing these amenities such that they have minimal impact on the budget.

Chapter 4
Finding the Right General Contractor

It is up to you, the homeowner, to ensure that you choose the right professional for the job. After all, the safety and wellbeing of your family is at stake.

You would never buy a car without taking it for a test drive, would you? The same rule holds true when choosing a contractor for your construction project. You need to do your homework and find out as much as possible about each contractor.

Quality contractors realize that this is how things are done, so they expect an interview; they expect that as a homeowner, you will want to shop around for a contractor who will work for them. If a contractor seems offended by this, then that's probably a sign he or she does not have your best interests at heart.

The General Contractor's Job
A general contractor has many responsibilities and duties. If I had to give one overarching description, I'd say that he or she is like the orchestra conductor.

Just as the conductor knows exactly when to bring in different sections of the orchestra, a general contractor knows exactly when to bring in each trade such that the job flows unimpeded. Just as the conductor knows exactly how each piece of music will sound, the contractor can see all the way through to the end of the project and what it's going to look like.

Contractors also bring specialized knowledge, skill, and their team of subcontractors.

Locating Contractors

So first things first—where do you go to find contractors in your area? Here are some ideas:

- Ask friends, family and neighbors for referrals.
- Many people start their search online
- Attend a "Tour of Homes" event and meet contractors and see their work.
- Call your local homebuilders' association.
- Look in the phone book.

Once you have a detailed outline of the job you want done, start calling contractors. If you have to leave a message, offer your name, contact info, the general area where you live, and the basics of what you want done. If you are able to talk to a contractor on the first try, or if he or she calls back, go ahead and offer further details about what you would like done. Depending on the contractor, he or she may offer a soft bid over the phone or will want to meet to discuss your project in person.

Response is Key

Perhaps the main complaint that I hear from clients is that they call contractors to bid, and then they never receive a return call. I recently was talking to a client that I prepared a bid for, and at the conclusion of the presentation I asked him if the price was within the scope of his the budget.

He told me that I was the first contractor to bid, and he really didn't know what the budget should be; he added at that he had two other contractors that he was expecting bids from, but they were not returning his calls.

Think about this for a moment: if you couldn't get them to call you back to bid the job, what would it be like if they were actually on the job? Calling people back that want to give you work is a no-brainer in my opinion. So if this happens to you, then just forget about those contractors and call others who will respond. That first response can say a lot about a contractor.

Here is what one of our clients had to say about our initial telephone response:

Michael Baum is wonderful to work with. He answered the phone on my first call, and within a week he had visited the project and prepared a very detailed and professional estimate." Cathy M.

Interviewing & Observing the Contractor

The interview process actually starts as soon as you make the first call to the contractor. Don't be afraid to ask a lot of questions, but also just observe how the person acts and conducts business.

How quickly he answers and returns the call, if at all? Did you get a live person? Did you have to go through multiple menus on a voicemail to leave a message or did you talk to someone?

At the appointment, observe if he or she arrived on time, and if not, did he or she call you to let you know they would be late? Once they arrived was he or she prepared for the meeting? Were they comfortable being interviewed?

The answers to these questions can you view a pretty good indication as to how that person operates. The way people communicate at the initial contact is the way that they're going to communicate during the entire process.

One question to consider is the person's position in the company. Is that person an actual principal of the company, or are they a salesperson? It has been my experiences that salesman sometimes tend to overpromise in order to sign the job. That can lead to serious issues once the job starts. The majority of my personal clients have told me that they prefer to deal with a principal and not a salesperson.

Next, determine this: is the person someone that you trust? Are they reliable, and are they someone that you can communicate with? How are their communication skills? Can they explain things in clear language not using construction jargon? This can be extremely important during the job. When a contractor looks at a set of plans, he knows what it's going to look like when complete. That is not a skill that most clients have, so the contractor needs to be able to communicate that to the client.

Reducing Remodel Stress
Another thing to consider is stress. Doe the potential contractor possess a personality that is calm in demeanor? Construction can be a highly stressful situation. The fact is, many marriages have ended in divorce because of the stress created during a prolonged construction project.

Results from an exclusive national survey by ServiceMagic.com of nearly 700 homeowners and 260 remodeling contractors show that prolonged projects can lead to tension:

- 78% of home remodeling professionals witnessed an argument between a couple either in the planning stage or during a home remodel project in the last year.
- On a scale of 1 to 10, (one being the lowest and 10 being the highest), stress levels for the homeowner's reach an astonishingly high average of 8 during the remodeling process.
- 64% of remodeling professionals say they witnessed an argument between their clients and had to play the role of relationship counselor.
- 79% of remodeling professionals have walked away from a work order because of excessive client arguing at some time in their careers.
- 69% of home remodels most significantly affect the stress levels of the mother or wife in the household.
- 82% of professionals said that a kitchen remodel is the project that causes the most stress among homeowners.

- Reassuringly, after the remodeling project is completed, 60% of couples' relationships sprang back to normal and became exponentially less stressful.

Temporary Move Out

While we are talking about stress, I would like to discuss clients living in their homes during the remodel. During my career I have done many major remodels, jobs that touched every room in the house.

From the contractor's perspective, having a client's personal possessions and the client still in the house during a major remodel makes the job more expensive, it takes longer, and it increases the stress level on every one.

Typically the furniture has to be moved multiple times, and it must be protected so it is covered and recovered. With clients living in the house, work has to be done in phases. It's difficult to get maximum work efficiency and unfortunately the contractor has to charge more to cover these costs.

For the homeowner, it is stressful and dirty, and with different workmen there, sometimes it feels like you're being invaded. Ultimately it's a bit like camping out in your own house.

Years ago I did a job that required that the roof be torn off, a second story built, and every room in the house remodeled. The husband, his wife, five-year-old son, and six- month-old infant lived in the house during the entire remodel. For the last month and a half of the job they all lived in one room. I spoke with him after the job was complete, and he admitted that staying in the house had been a mistake. Obviously there are circumstances, budget issues, maybe even pet issues that might preclude someone from moving out.

My advice is, if at all possible, temporarily move out. It's worth it.

Contractor Communication

Choosing someone that you can relate to and communicate with even when things are stressful is essential. There is an analogy that a construction project can be like taking a trip with someone. If you like the people you're traveling with, the journey is much more enjoyable, even if there are a few bumps along the way. But if you do not like that person, it doesn't matter where you go—the journey will not be pleasant.

Please approach with caution any contractor that says he can start on your job tomorrow. For a lot of people, the main criterions for choosing a contractor is when they can start the job. It is a fact of life for contractors to have clients that cancel jobs just prior to the start, leaving an opening in their schedule. You want to make sure that this is the case and not because he or she simply has no work.

Next, find out what kind of experience each contractor has. Find out their story. How did they get into the business, how long they been doing contracting, what types of jobs do they specialize in? Do they like doing what they do? See if their passion for the job shows through.

Ask about continuing education. Do they stay current on the newest trends and technologies? For instance, are they familiar with Smart Home technology? Are they associated with any local or national trade associations?

How do they stay in contact during job—by phone, by text, by email? Are they readily available for communication should you need them? I am always available by phone, text, and email. I always respond promptly. My clients really appreciate being able to get answers to their questions immediately.

Another thing you would want to know is, do they educate the clients as they go about the project? Here is a testimonial from one of our clients regarding educating them:

"The best thing about working with him is he outlined the entire project and gives clear details on the step-by-step construction. He took my suggestions on things I wanted done" Mitra R.

Construction, especially after demolition is started, is an ominous and scary experience for someone who has never undertaken construction before. I have a regular weekly meeting set up with each of my clients to go over progress on each project, answer any questions, and explain what to expect next and avoid any surprises for my clients; this also serves to relieve some of fear of the unknown for them.

While surprises can be exciting and wonderful in some aspects of life, it's not something that you really want to experience regularly during a remodeling project.

After you interview all of your contractors, I suggest that you make calls to each of them maybe on several occasions to see if they respond in the same way they did on the initial contact.

Contractor Interviewing Homeowner
Be aware that the interview process is a two-way street. While you are interviewing the contractor, the contractor will be interviewing you. There seems to be a premise out there that contractors will take any work you put in front of them; while that may be true for less successful contractors, the ones that are successful take on jobs with people that they like, and the jobs that are inside their core competencies. Typically these contractors will have a back log of work and they are much more selective about who they work with.

Construction is a business, and like everyone, we enjoy working with people we like to be around. In my career I have turned down good jobs simply because I thought that working with the particular client was not going to be an enjoyable experience.

Chapter 5
Checking the Contractor's Background

While talking and meeting with a contractor is very important, it is still important to verify the contractor's background. He or she may have told you they are licensed and insured, but don't take their word for it; do your homework now and avoid costly mistakes later.

Only choose licensed, bonded, and insured contractors with an extensive work history and plenty of satisfied customers as references. To ensure that you make the best choice in a contractor, whether you're looking to add a room, remake that 1970s kitchen, or provide you with emergency repair work, you'll need to know what qualities a good contractor should have.

Here are the top things to look for when hiring a general contractor:

- licensing (current and state-specific)
- insurance (liability & workman's compensation
- bonded (many states require contractors to be bonded)
- competitive pricing (note that this doesn't mean ("cheapest")
- long history of satisfied customers provided as references
- willing to sign a contract with a detailed scope of work
- listed with your city/county chamber of commerce (possibly the better business bureau)
- willing to provide you with a written estimate and sit through an interview
- verified through the contractor's license board or state attorney general and is a member of local/state trade organizations
- provides sound advice concerning your construction/addition/remodeling plans in accordance with your goals and high quality build
- accepts credit cards as well as cash and checks
- gets building permits for you

- offers a reasonable warranty (neither too short/ nor exceptionally longer than average)

References

Speak with prior clients and find out what their experience was like. Visit other homes where the contractor has worked and inspect the quality of the finished job. Here are some important questions to ask when checking references:

a. Would you rehire the contractor?
b. Were they easy to communicate / work with?
c. Was the job completed on schedule? If not why?
d. Were there significant cost overruns?
e. Were the cost overruns driven by changes to the scope of work?
f. Were the materials used to your specifications?
g. Were corrections/changes made in a timely manner?
h. Were you satisfied with the quality, cost and time required for completion?
i. Did the contractor adhere to the terms spelled out in the contract?
j. Did the contractor listen to your concerns?

Better Business Bureau

The Better Business Bureau (BBB) is a private company that rates businesses. While I agree that this should be a company that you contact when you are looking for contractors, however, it should not be the deciding factor. The only way you can be rated by the BBB is to pay them to be a member. I'm sure there are plenty of companies out there that are very reputable but are not members of the Better Business Bureau.

License

Currently only Florida, Louisiana, Colorado, Connecticut, Kansas, Indiana, Missouri, New Hampshire, New York, Ohio, Pennsylvania and Wyoming don't require a specific state license for contractors. And even in some of those states there are certain conditions when jobs reach a dollar threshold a contractor's license are then required.

Not only should they be licensed, it is up to you to verify that fact. The number of homeowners who do not verify the contractor's license is surprising. Anyone can claim to be a licensed contractor, but that does not make it so. Make sure you ask to see the contractor's license, ensure that it is not expired, and that it is from your state (out of state licenses are not valid). You can also double check licensing online.

Be aware, there is going to be a huge temptation to use someone without a license that has been referred to you by someone you trust in order to save money. I have saying in my bid documents, "if you think it's expensive to hire professional, wait until you hire an amateur." My firm has been hired to come in and repair work from unlicensed contractors on many occasions. This is really something you want to avoid, as you run the risk of having to pay for the job twice.

In the state of California for residential construction, there are General Contractor's licenses— called B licenses—and then there are individual or specialty licenses such as concrete, electrical, or plumbing—those are C licenses. These are the contractors you would be dealing with should you decide to act as your own general contractor

Insurance

The contractor that you choose should have insurance coverage for himself and his crew. In my state, these are called general liability and workman's compensation insurance. If he doesn't, you <u>must</u> find another contractor.

Should an accident or injury happen on the job, your homeowner's insurance would be responsible for the claim. <u>If</u> they pay the claim, this could dramatically increase your rates for no good reason—the contractor should always have his or her own insurance policy, and you should verify that fact prior to hiring. The insurance policy is also source of reimbursement should the contractor not do proper work. If the contractor does not carry insurance it also puts him at a competitive advantage over all of the contractors who do carry the proper insurance.

When verifying insurance, please make sure that it is still in effect during the course of the job. I've heard of circumstances where unethical contractors have given homeowners certificates of insurance that were no longer in effect, or that might expire during the job leaving the homeowner unprotected.

Brand / Reputation

What was it about the company that attracted you to them? Was it their reputation, was it a referral from a trusted source, or was it advertising?

Were they perhaps working in your neighborhood? Do they have a website? Have you been to it?

Does the contractor have a third-party survey company that they work with, such as Guild Quality, to elicit honest feedback from clients? We use Guild Quality and have found that our clients like the fact that we want to know how we are performing for them.

Is the contractor part of a nationwide network of service providers such as Angie's List or Service Magic? If so how are they rated?

Do they have an online presence such as Twitter, LinkedIn, or Facebook? Have you checked their online references with sites like Yelp etc.?

Have they had any complaints, and if so how did they handle them? As a consumer if I find only great reviews, I begin to wonder if the company is cherry picking testimonials. It would be a rare company that has only rave reviews.

Guarantees

A guarantee is a promise to fulfill on a commitment that you made to someone. Unfortunately, too many bad contractors out there don't fulfill their promises. Here are some nightmares that are all too common:

- Rumors abound about contractors that took deposits and never came back.
- The job took longer than they said it would take.
- The job cost more than they said would cost.
- They left my house a mess.

These complaints and validated by a survey from ServiceMagic.com that indicates that stress levels during the construction process are significantly increased due to three main sources of frustration:

- 42% say the remodel took longer than they wished.
- 39% say their contractor was messy.
- 33% say the project went over budget.

In order to alleviate these complaints, my company offers a four part guarantee; we guarantee no down payment upfront, we guarantee the construction schedule and we pay the client should we fail to meet that schedule, we guarantee the budget as long as no changes are made, and we guarantee that we will leave the house spotless upon completion.

Warrantees

A warranty is a promise to repair or correct any item that might become a problem in the future. For instance, my company provides a written one year unlimited warranty on all work that we do.

It is important to know exactly what the contractor is going to stand behind once the job is complete. The only way that you know and can enforce this is to have a written warranty. Having this gives you peace of mind should anything happen in regards to your construction project. Make sure to get any warrantees in writing. Make them an addendum to the contract!

Long but Important Process

You may be thinking that interviewing and checking the backgrounds of multiple contractors will be too time consuming, and you don't even have any bids yet! But it is important to be patient. This is how the process should be done. While it will take extra time, in the end finding a quality contractor who you can trust and work with will be worth the extra effort.

Chapter 6
Bids & Contracts

Now comes the part you've been waiting for—bids and contracts. You may think this is pretty cut and dry, but there is a lot to consider. Each contractor may have their own way of doing things. So it's your job to sort it all out to make sure you are getting the best information possible.

Gathering Bids

During the interview process, be sure to discuss what form their bid will be in; is it very detailed or is it more general? There are two schools of thought in this matter. Some contractors like to keep scope of work in their bids vague. Other contractors prefer to have everything detailed and clear from the very beginning.

During the interview, you should ask if their bid is based on actual fixtures such as plumbing, electrical, and appliances, or are they giving you an allowance for you to choose your own?

Someone who has never worked with a contractor before does not know whether the amount of the allowance will be sufficient to purchase the level of fixtures that they are anticipating. To overcome this issue, I actually include photographs and prices of the fixtures I'm proposing in my bid documents.

Getting bids from contractors can be a time-consuming and sometimes a frustrating process. It can involve waiting as contractors can be busy and it might take some time for him or her to provide an estimate. It is imperative that you get "apples for apples" bids from all your potential contractors. If one contractor leaves out a major component, his or her bid will appear to be the best bid only to surprise you later with a change order.

Also take this into consideration: as a homeowner, you may start out and with a clear idea of what you want. And upon the first contractor visiting, the job site new ideas arise. When the next contractor shows up those ideas are then incorporated into the scope of work for that contractor, and so on. The best way to proceed is to have everyone bid on the same thing; so make sure you have everything (your most final version) in writing present to each contractor. By engaging an architect or designer for the project, most of this can be worked out prior to the bidding process. This is the only way to ensure that you will obtain "apples for apples" bids.

It can be tempting to go with the first offer you get, but that could be a bad move. Make sure you get bids from several different contractors prior to making a hiring decision (3 bids should typically be obtained). By obtaining multiple bids, you will be able to compare offers and contractors, and then make the best decision for your needs.

Lowest Doesn't Always Mean Best

It can also be tempting to choose the lowest bid, but that could be a serious mistake. The lowest bid could mean substantial change orders. The lowest cost does not necessarily mean the best professional for the job. While you should certainly have a firm budget in place, you should not sacrifice quality, peace of mind and safety in an effort to save a few dollars. The price should be a factor, but you need to consider much more before making a decision. You should also ask yourself if you feel comfortable with the contractor being around your home and family and if his price is competitive (rather than rock bottom).

Remember that a contractor who has incredibly low prices might not be around when you need him in the future. You need to choose a professional with whom you can forge a lasting relationship, not one who will take your money and not be there when you need them in the future.

A couple of years ago, a prospective client wanted to do a major remodel/addition on his house. It involved removing and replacing the entire front of the two-story house, adding two bedrooms and two bathrooms, remodeling two existing bathrooms and a new kitchen— a total remodel. At the bid presentation, the owner told me that he needed to be at a certain price. Since that was my cost for the job, we did not end up doing the project. He went with the low bid contractor. At the presentation, I had guaranteed that the job would be done in 16 weeks. The contractor that he went with took six months to complete the project and ultimately it cost him almost $100,000 more to complete the project. Low bid does not equal best bid!

Let's talk about contracting philosophies. The one I described above is called *low-balling.* That's when a contractor intentionally comes in with a low price in order to get the job knowing full well that not everything has been included in the contract. That means that the contractor is going to be coming back to the client to get additional monies for "extras" (things not covered in the contract). Typically by the time one of these contractors is done, the cost of the job is as high or higher than the others that were bidding.

The downside to the client is, it costs more to get rid of that contractor and hire another one then it is to pay the extra costs. The worst part is it results in a bad experience for the consumer. They feel like they are being held hostage. We've all heard stories of someone who was taken advantage of by a contractor. I would like to say that low balling not a common practice, but it is.

The lowest price usually does not necessarily equate to quality work, either. Contractors who are willing to undercut the competition by a substantial amount often cut corners in the construction process – they might use lower grade materials or hire workers without the necessary experience for a high quality build.

Recently I was told by a potential client that her friend had contracted for a kitchen remodel. After starting the job, the contractor came to his client said that he had under bid the job and needed more money. A short time later he came back to the client and again asked for more money. This time she said no, the contractor has since walked off of the job leaving it incomplete. The client had paid in good faith but was left with a partially finished kitchen that she could not use and had to start the process over with this experience as her view of all contractors.

The bottom dollar option is rarely a good solution, even when you need work done in a hurry. There's an old saying and unfortunately it usually holds true: "you can get good work, you can get cheap work, but you can't get good cheap work."

The other philosophy is called a *turn-key* bid, which means everything that needs to be in the contract is included; that allows the owners know exactly how much they're going to be spending on the project. I tell my clients that if they decided to go on vacation for the duration of the job, when they got back their house would be completely ready to live in, right down to the final cleaning.

Regardless of the price of the job, the form in which the bid is delivered in can vary greatly. There will be an example of a bid or scope of work later on in the book.

Most contractors have an expiration date on their bid. Please discuss with each contractor: how long their bid is good for? The cost of materials and labor to the contractor changes all the time. Many materials such as copper wire, copper pipe, drywall, and lumber are commodities that fluctuate the with the commodities markets. The labor portion of the subcontractors bids change based on the amount of work going on in each locality. If everyone is busy, labor prices go up!

Contracts

Some homeowners feel that a written contract is not really necessary. You might even think that it's a waste of time; someone you trust referred this person so just a handshake and verbal agreement should suffice, right?

Actually, not having a contract is not only wrong, it can be very expensive. You should <u>always</u> make sure that you have a written contract in place. This protects both you and the contractor, and more than likely be required by your state, as well.

When you think about it, contracts don't really matter if everything goes well. But what if it doesn't? Make sure you read the contract. Make sure it is not written in such a manner that one party has more power than the other.

In addition to the initial contract, make sure that any changes to the scope on the project are added to the contract. The contract should spell out exactly what is included in the job, down to the materials used and even the model number for specific items. A high level of specificity in the scope of work avoids many problems later on.

Decide on a process for completion of your project. Some firms use a "final punch list" method, whereby the client and contactor walk the job and agree on items that need to be corrected and a schedule of when they will be completed. Once accomplished, the project is deemed complete. Other firms use a more organic process, where the client informs the contractor of any issues while the work is on-going and corrections are made at the time.

Set the expectations for everyone from the very beginning with transparency and clarity. The contract should also include information about payment, how changes to the plans will be handled and what steps must be followed by both parties in the event of a cancellation.

Chapter 7
Hiring Your Chosen Contractor

You've received bids, you've interviewed and observed contractors, and now you're ready to hire your chosen contractor. Congrats! Now it's time to sit down with your contractor and iron out the details of your project.

Working with Your Contractor

The more information that you can get settled and clarified up front, the smoother the project is going to run. It is imperative that you work out how the communication is going to work between you and your contractor. Are you going to have a regular meeting? Are you going to talk on the phone every day? What is the process going to look like?

It seems like a pretty basic thing to ask, but is he going to have workers on the job every day? Does he guarantee the completion date? What happens if there is a problem over the weekend? Who do you call? For instance, if it's a plumbing leak, do you call the plumber directly or call the contractor?

Many people that I've spoken with that have had a bad experience with a contractor told me that there were days and sometimes a week at a time when no one would show up on the job, then all kinds of people would show up, coincidentally just in time for the next payment.

Partnership

Over the years I've experienced many relationships with clients. The ones that have worked the best are the ones where we were in partnership together. A remodel or addition is a major undertaking, and you have selected a contractor for his or her knowledge, experience and expertise, but there are still decisions that you will need to be a part of. As partners, you should have ongoing discussions about what is happening on the project.

I have also had clients that were very successful in their individual areas of expertise that thought that their expertise carried over to management of their project. They tended to be micro-managers and had difficulty letting me run the project. They constantly questioned the order of things with no experience or knowledge as to how a typical construction project runs. During these projects, I felt like I was spending more time explaining what I was doing or about to do than I was actually doing it. You've hired a professional—let him do his job. Trust but verify.

Permits
By state law as a licensed contractor, I'm required to pull permits on every project. As a homeowner you will want to have permits on any construction you do at your home, especially if you're adding square footage to the house. When you sell your house, if you have not gotten a permit you will not get credit for that square footage from an appraiser. From the homeowners' perspective the downside is that you will get a supplemental tax bill for the improvements and your property taxes will go up. If you don't there is also the possibility the Code Enforcement could require you tear down any unpermitted work or pay extra for not getting a permit at the time of remodel.

Make your contractor responsible for pulling all permits. If you pull them as a homeowner, your contractor has no responsibility for the job as far as the city is concerned. Also make him responsible for meeting with the inspector for each inspection.

I've had several clients tell me that on previous jobs they were responsible for meeting the inspector and getting the inspections. That left the contractor available to be on someone else's job. In my opinion, that is wrong on so many levels. When an inspector comes to the jobsite, they are expecting to see a professional that knows what's going on and can explain it. If they have a technical question and the homeowner cannot answer it, it can result in project delays, and lastly it sends a message to the client that the other client's job is more important than their job. That is bad form and bad business.

Buying Materials

During the research portion of your project, you will undoubtedly be looking at pricing at the big box stores such as Home Depot and Lowe's. I've had a number of clients ask me why my pricing is more expensive then the big box stores. The answer is that the price that the big box stores charge does not include somebody going there, purchasing it, bringing it back to the jobsite and being responsible for it until it is installed and then warranting it once it is.

That brings up the issue of homeowners wanting to purchase materials for the job. I've worked a couple of projects where the homeowners wanted to supply materials to try to avoid the markup that a contractor charges. The problem is that they don't buy the correct material, they don't buy enough of the correct material, or the material is not on the job when needed.

For example, I had a client that supplied all of the finish materials including the electrical plugs and switches. She assured me that all these items were at the house in the correct quantity. It ended up that the client had not bought enough material. I ended up having to pay standing time to keep a five man electrical crew on the job while she went and bought more.

As I mentioned earlier, one of the guarantees that I commit to is that if I do not complete the job on time, I pay the client for each day until it is complete. In order to meet this goal I must have control over all of the parts and pieces of the project. That is why I require that I supply the all of the materials for a project.

Hiring Your Own Subcontractors

One of the primary reasons that you hire a general contractor is to the access to his subcontractors. Pretty regularly I've had people ask me if they could bring in their brother-in-law, uncle, father, or someone they know who is a tradesman or subcontractor to do a portion of the job in order to save money. I have agreed to this twice and both times it has been disastrous. It delayed the project by weeks. Since their loyalty was to the client, I had no influence or pull with them to adhere to my schedule.

Contractors build relationships with their subcontractors over long periods of time. The subcontractors know what to expect from the general contractor and vice versa. Bringing someone that is not known into the mix is a recipe for problems. The relationship and loyalty between general contractor and subcontractors goes beyond business; they become a team moving from job to job.

Just as any high-performing team would be hesitant to bring a player on that they've never worked with, it's the same with the general contractor in his subcontractors. If I am responsible for the outcome of the job, then I want to rely on people that I know can get the job done.

Doing Some of the Work Yourself

The next issue that comes up is that the homeowner wants to do part of the job himself. Personally this is usually a deal breaker for me. This goes back to guaranteeing the delivery date. Part of the cost on the project is based how long the contractor is going to be there supervising. If a contractor has to wait for the client to complete some portion of the work, that means the contractor must expend more time on supervision than planned, and they can't go on to the next job. I hope that as you read this book you can see it from the contractor's perspective and understand the reasoning behind this.

Selections

No matter what type of remodeling you're planning, there are great many selections that need to be made: things like baseboards, casings, crown molding, tile, windows, granite, paint color, wall texture, carpet, plumbing fixtures, light fixtures, appliances, door styles, and cabinets. By making sure all of the selections are made prior to starting your job, you give will give your contractor the maximum time to source and coordinate the delivery of all of these finishes.

I once had an out-of-state client who took a month to choose the carpet and paint colors. Needless to say, it impacted the project timeline negatively. Rather than leave this totally up to the homeowner to take care of, I provide my clients with an hour of interior design consultation for free, a $300 value. Over 50% of my clients are able to make their selections in that first meeting; the ones who can't engage the interior designer and work with her directly until complete.

Work Schedule

Decide on the work schedule in advance of the job start. The start and stop times each day should be predictable, especially if one of the clients is staying at home during the project. The contractor should try to accommodate the schedule of the clients as best as they can.

In my company, we typically start work at 8 a.m. and end at 4 p.m. that allows the homeowner's family time to get up and get ready each day.

Another question that comes up is about Saturday work. We try not to work on Saturdays if possible but do on occasion, with the permission of the client. Having people in your house all week is quite an intrusion, and it is nice to have the weekend off.

Payment

Cash flow is the lifeblood of any business. The faster a contractor gets paid, the more motivation they have to complete the job quickly. As a side note, I do not believe in large deposits prior to starting the job. In my state, $1000 is the maximum amount a contractor can charge as a deposit.

Work out payments in the beginning. I do not invoice until we reach a predetermined milestone of work that has been completed. By the time I invoice the client, I've already accrued monies owed to my subcontractors and suppliers. Be prepared to make payments promptly upon receipt of invoices. I can't think of anything that would make your contractor happier. However I am not advocating paying for work before it's done.

Milestones for Payment

I recommend using the milestone payment method. The milestone method is simply that the contractor must achieve completion of a phase of the project prior to getting paid. This protects you the consumer from the contractor "getting ahead of you" on payments.

Here is an example of typical milestone payment schedule that I use for a remodel / addition: Each milestone is preceded by a dollar amount so the client knows how much is due upon completion of each milestone and can plan accordingly.

$Draw upon issue of Building Permits & Mobilization
$Draw upon completion of Demolition
$Draw upon completion of Rough Framing
$Draw upon completion of Rough Electrical
$Draw upon completion of Rough Plumbing
$Draw upon completion of Insulation
$Draw upon completion of Drywall
$Draw upon completion of Stucco
$Draw upon completion of Ceramic Tile
$Draw upon completion of Interior Doors & Trim
$Draw upon completion of Painting
$Draw upon completion of Cabinets
$Draw upon completion of Countertops
$Draw upon completion of Finish Plumbing
$Draw upon completion of Flooring
$Draw upon Substantial Completion

While doing a job for some clients, I was told "the *last contractor we had would come to us the day before and tell us that he needed x dollars tomorrow, to pay his guys. Then we had to make that happen.*" In doing so, this contractor was making them responsible for his payroll. Please remember this, "the contractor's payroll is not your problem or responsibility." The milestone payment schedule alleviates this issue from ever coming up.

Final Payment
Final payment should not be made unless you are satisfied that all corrections have been made. This is not a time to pay and hope that the contractor comes back to make the repairs.

If it is a large amount and the corrections are minor, I think it is justified to pay the contractor a fair amount. For instance, there is $1,000 worth of corrections to be made and you are holding $10,000, I think it's fair to pay the contractor $8,000-$9,000 pending completion. Make sure the project's official closeout is discussed prior to signing a contract.

In my contract, I base the final payment on Substantial Completion. We like to take care of any corrections as they are noted by my clients so that at completion the list of correction is small. If you don't know what Substantial Completion is, here is my definition: "The date on which the building or a specified portion is complete and can be occupied or used for its intended purpose in accordance with contract and/or regulatory requirements." I adopted this process because I've had clients in the past that, for whatever reason, did not want to get a final inspection on their project even though they were already living in the room addition or remodeled room.

Pets
Pets can add interesting dimension to a construction project. I've worked on projects with both dogs and cats. A simple instruction like "keep the gate closed" can easily get screwed up on a construction project. You're probably wondering, how?

Each day different contractors show up at the job, and it's possible that they might even have different people on their crew. Their focus is on what has to be done that day, so it's easy to not convey a simple instruction like "keep the gate closed."

I remember one job we spent almost two hours trying to catch a dog that had gotten out of the backyard. The message here is that the pets are your responsibility as an owner. Please don't put that on your contractor; make any arrangements necessary for your pets.

Customer Service

After so many years in business, completing the actual construction on-time and on-budget is the easy part of a project. Customer service is not something that happens after the job is complete; it should be present during the entire process.

When I start working with a new client I'm not only focused on that job, I want to earn the right to be their trusted contractor for life. I operate my business on a philosophy that marketing guru Jay Abraham describes as "Preeminence." While most businesses are focused on selling a product or service, *my focus is to become my client's most trusted advisor, to care more about them than I care about making the sale.*

There have been times when I have advised clients to not do a particular project because I didn't think they would get a large enough return on their investment. When something is happening with their house I want their first call to be to me. That gives me an opportunity to advise and guide them even if there is no monetary gain in it for me.

I've spoken with several potential clients who previously had remodeling done prior to contacting us; and they told me that they couldn't wait to get the contractor out of their house. It saddened me a bit to hear that. Clearly those companies were focused on getting the job done and getting paid, and not caring about or satisfying the client. Here is what one of our client's said about us regarding this:

"Please don't change! What Baum has is working. My husband and I and so many bad experiences with other contractors, Baum is a breath of fresh air! Tuesday c

I also try to make it fun. I tease and joke with my clients whenever we meet. Remodeling is stressful enough already; I don't want to make it worse. Especially if something unexpected happens.

In the back of the book there is a wonderful note that we received from a young couple and their son. Although his Mom had to do the writing, Noah's note about growing up in that house touched me. I think that most contractors treat the house like a worksite and forget that it is also someone's home. When I think about it that way, it gives me a whole new context and approach to each project.

I said earlier that we give a written unlimited one year warranty on our work. However that doesn't mean after one year we forget about them. If a client calls me with a problem, I go look at it whether it had something to do with our work or not.

I recall one time a client we had previously done a remodel for called me after two years to tell me that a light switch was not working. Clearly it was beyond the 1 year warranty but I went out and replaced it. That's what I mean about wanting to be the first call that my clients make.

As much as it pains me to admit it, there are unscrupulous contractors out there. They *lowball* the bid in order to get the job and then come after their client for additional monies. I'm going to paint with a broad brush now, but typically those are the same contractors that when something goes wrong, they are not around. Suddenly they no longer answer your calls.

I have a name for these guys; I call them "Chuck in the Truck." Usually they have no office, they have no staff, and when you call them with the problem they're no longer "available." As a consumer, you want to make sure that the contractor you hire is going to be around should any issues come up.

The goal and mission of my company is *100% satisfaction for every client, provide an extraordinary customer experience and to receive a referral.* That should be the level of service that <u>you</u> should demand of <u>your</u> contractor.

Additional Assistance

Home remodeling projects can become fairly complex in nature. Because of this, many homeowners prefer to seek the guidance of a proven authority to answer their remodeling questions along the way—and to have someone in their corner to guide them through their projects.

To meet that important need, I offer consulting services to help homeowners skip the common frustrations of "trial and error" and the expensive mistakes and delays that can easily occur in remodeling projects.

For General Contractors, I offer consulting to assist them with their questions, as well as assist them to streamline their business processes.

In either case, to skip the learning curve and to take advantage of many years worth of remodeling experience, I encourage you to contact me at: http://sawdusttosatisfaction.com/consulting.

If you are planning a remodel in the greater Long Beach area of Southern California, let's get together, and I will bid your upcoming project. I provide a comprehensive bid that you will be glad to have, and I provide an exclusive four-part guarantee that you will not find from another local general contractor.

Please contact me here:

Michael Baum
Baum Construction & Development
(562) 42-4Baum (2286)
mbaum@baumcon.com
http://BaumCon.com

Chapter 8
Top Remodeling Projects with the Best Return on Your Investment

There are tons of ways to change your home to better suit your needs. However, they're not all equal in terms of what you'll gain back from them. Some remodeling projects offer a much better return on your investment.

If you decide to put your home on the market in the future knowing what the highest returning remodeling projects are will help you.

Following are some photos of our past projects as examples.

Kitchen Remodeling

Perhaps the most commonly remodeled room in the home, the kitchen is an ideal place to start work for those with an eye for better usability, style, and better resale value.

You can choose to go with a smaller or larger scale remodel shown in the photo here. You might opt to resurface your cabinets and add new appliances, or you might choose to replace the flooring, countertops, lighting order to complete kitchen.

Expect a return of 80 to 98 percent, depending on what you do and what your market is like. Following are some photos of work I have completed.

Bathroom Remodeling

The bathroom is another prime area for remodeling. Changing out the old tub and worn out vanity, replacing your faucets and adding new lighting can add up to a significantly more appealing bathroom.

You'll find this is perhaps the highest returning remodeling project for your home, with a national average of 102 percent return for most remodeling jobs.

Exterior Remodeling

Remodeling your home doesn't have to include adding a new room or ripping out your old outdated fixtures. It can be as simple as adding new vinyl siding to the outside of your home or even a fresh coat of paint to tired wood siding.

Exterior work can offer a return of hundred percent depending on what you in the area in which your home is located.

New Family Room

Sometimes going bigger is really the only way to make sure that you and your family have the space that you need. One of the more common remodeling projects is to add a family room to your home, typically one about 16 x 25.

Depending on the flooring you use, you can expect to see a return of about 81% with a new family room should you decide to sell your home.

Adding a Deck

According to many realtors, one of the best additions to your home in terms of cost versus potential return is a deck the simple wood deck can cost very little to complete, but can have a big impact on the resale value of your home, as well as the speed with which you are able to sell it should you put it on the market. Having a deck also offers an immediate return for your family, that can't be measured in dollars.

Landscaping Options

Landscaping your yard offers many of the same benefits as remodeling the exterior of your home. Namely, it helps you make a better first impression on potential buyers. Landscaping projects can also make your home more beautiful for your family, more usable and even more kid friendly.

Basement Remodeling

Another excellent remodeling project is to finish out that basement. Perhaps you put in an in-law suite, or a bar and game room. Finishing out your basement adds usable space to your home, increasing your marketable square footage and can make your home a more appealing option for buyers.

The national average is a return value of about 77 percent with a basement remodel, though that certainly depends on what you do with that space.

In the photos below this basement was transformed into a cozy family room.

Detailed Scope of Work
Miscellaneous Remodeling To Include:

Kitchen
Demo cabinets and wet bar area.
Supply and install new stain grade riff cut white oak cabinets with slab doors
Supply and install Caesarstone "Haze 2030" countertops. Square edge.
Supply and install Kohler executive chef K-5931-4U-0 under mount sink.
Supply and install New Delta Linden 4353T-DST 8 inch installation kitchen faucet, no soap dispenser.
Supply and install four recessed LED lights.
Supply and install sliding pocket door at pantry. One light white lami glass.
Supply and install Neos Tile "Silver" porcelain tile flooring.
Install owner's appliances.

Dining Room
Supply and install Neos Tile "Silver" porcelain tile flooring.
Supply and install four recessed LED lights.
Supply and install sliding pocket door to kitchen.
Supply and install glass partition at entry.
Remove acoustic ceiling .

Living Room
Supply and install Neos Tile "Silver" porcelain tile flooring.
Fill in "pit" at living room.
Remove acoustic ceiling.

Powder Bath
Remove existing cabinets.
Supply and install riff cut white oak cabinets with slab doors.

Supply and install Kohler Verticyl Rectangle Sink K-2882-0.
Supply and install Moen 90 Degree S6700 Faucet Finish CP.
Supply and install Caesar stone "Haze 2030" countertops. Square edge.
Supply and install Neos Tile "Silver" porcelain tile flooring.

Laundry
Supply and install Neos Tile "Silver" porcelain tile flooring.
Supply and install in-wall laundry box.
Re-locate dryer vent to exterior.

Bedroom 1
Supply and install Cascade Series alpine engineered maple flooring.
Supply and install two recessed LED lights.
Remove existing ceiling fan.

Upstairs Hall
Supply and install Cascade Series alpine engineered maple flooring.

Hall Bath
Supply and install new Kohler Archer 60x30 K-1946-RA-0 Tub W K-7272-CP ClearFlo slotted overflow drain.
Supply and install Kohler Stance Ritetemp K-T14776-4-CP tub/shower valve and trim.
Supply and install new ceramic tile surrounds. Tile to 6'0".
Supply and install new 5'6" riff cut white oak cabinets with slab doors.
Supply and install Kohler Verticyl rectangle sink K-2882-0.
Supply and install Moen 90 degree S6700 faucet.
Supply and install Kohler K-6303-0 veil wall hung one piece toilet.
Supply and install Times Square beige porcelain tile flooring.
Supply and install LG Viatera "Sienna Sand" counter. Square edge.

Master Bedroom
Demo existing flat ceiling.

Supply and install mirrored wardrobe doors.
Supply and install Cascade Series alpine engineered maple flooring.

Master Bath
Supply and install Kohler Watertile K-8023-CP wall mounted square with soothing spray with Kohler Loure volume control K-T14671-4-CP tub/shower valve and trim.
Supply and install new Ceramic Tile Surrounds. Tile to 6'0".
Supply and install new 32" riff cut white oak cabinets with slab doors.
Supply and install Caesar stone Classico "Pure White 1141" counter. Edge detail square.
Supply and install Kohler Verticyl rectangle K-2882-0 sink.
Supply and install Moen 90 degree TS6720 BN faucet.
Supply and install Kohler K-6303-0 veil wall hung one piece toilet.
Supply and install Times Square beige porcelain tile flooring.
Supply and install sliding pocket door at Pantry. One light white lami-glass.

Bedroom 2
Supply and install Cascade Series alpine engineered maple flooring.
Supply and install wardrobe doors.

Bedroom 3
Supply and install Cascade Series alpine engineered maple flooring.
Supply and install wardrobe doors.

Misc.
Patch drywall as necessary for paint.
Re-ripe water system in PEX pipe.
Supply and install tankless water heater.
Supply and install new entry door and jamb, $3,000 allowance.
Supply and install new 200amp electrical service
Paint interior first floor. Color TBD.

Supply and install 31/2 inch base throughout house
Supply and install new laundry sink and garage.
Supply and install new steel and acrylic stairs at handrail.
Remove acoustic ceilings at first floor only.
Supply and install Brainerd 3 ¾ in Tribeca pulls at all cabinet.

	Prelim Budget	Actual Budget	Variance	Change Orders	Total Budget
ARCHITECTURAL	$0.00	$0.00	$0.00	0.00	0.00
STRUCTURAL ENGINEERING	$0.00	$0.00	$0.00	0.00	0.00
STRUCTURAL INSPECTIONS	$0.00	$0.00	$0.00	0.00	0.00
CIVIL ENGINEERING	$0.00	$0.00	$0.00	0.00	0.00
REPROGRAPHICS	$0.00	$0.00	$0.00	0.00	0.00
CONSULTANT	$0.00	$0.00	$0.00	0.00	0.00
LANDSCAPE ARCHITECT	$0.00	$0.00	$0.00	0.00	0.00
SOILS ENGINEER	$0.00	$0.00	$0.00	0.00	0.00
CONCRETE TESTING	$0.00	$0.00	$0.00	0.00	0.00
TRACT MAP FEES	$0.00	$0.00	$0.00	0.00	0.00
BONDS	$0.00	$0.00	$0.00	0.00	0.00
PLANCHECK FEES	$0.00	$0.00	$0.00	0.00	0.00
SCHOOL FEES	$0.00	$0.00	$0.00	0.00	0.00
BUILDING PERMITS	**$2,250.00**	$0.00	$2,250.00	0.00	2,250.00
SANITATION FEES	$0.00	$0.00	$0.00	0.00	0.00
WATER FEES	$0.00	$0.00	$0.00	0.00	0.00
TRAFFIC IMPACT FEES	$0.00	$0.00	$0.00	0.00	0.00
PARK FEES	$0.00	$0.00	$0.00	0.00	0.00
WATER METER	$0.00	$0.00	$0.00	0.00	0.00
UTILITY DEPOSITS	$0.00	$0.00	$0.00	0.00	0.00
TEMPORARY FACILITIES	$600.00	$0.00	$600.00	0.00	600.00
ASBESTOS SURVEY / REMOVAL	$0.00	$0.00	$0.00	0.00	0.00
LEAD PAINT PROCEDURE	$0.00	$0.00	$0.00	0.00	0.00
DEMO-SITE PREP.	$7,500.00	$0.00	$7,500.00	0.00	7,500.00
TRASH HAULING	$0.00	$0.00	$0.00	0.00	0.00
IMPORT / EXPORT	$1,200.00	$0.00	$1,200.00	0.00	1,200.00
EROSION CONTROL	$0.00	$0.00	$0.00	0.00	0.00
ONSITE STREETS	$0.00	$0.00	$0.00	0.00	0.00
OFFSITE WORK	$0.00	$0.00	$0.00	0.00	0.00
RETAINING WALLS	$0.00	$0.00	$0.00	0.00	0.00
CONCRETE / FOUNDATIONS	$5,650.00	$0.00	$5,650.00	0.00	5,650.00
STRUCT. STEEL	$0.00	$0.00	$0.00	0.00	0.00
PLUMBING-LABOR	$6,280.00	$0.00	$6,280.00	0.00	6,280.00
PLUMBING-FIXTURES	$0.00	$0.00	$0.00	0.00	0.00
TANKLESS WATERHEATER	$0.00	$0.00	$0.00	0.00	0.00
LUMBER-FRAMING	$7,175.00	$0.00	$7,175.00	0.00	7,175.00
CARPENTRY-FRAMING	$17,375.00	$0.00	$17,375.00	0.00	17,375.00
HARDWARE-FRAMING	$1,200.00	$0.00	$1,200.00	0.00	1,200.00
LUMBER SIDING / CAP	$0.00	$0.00	$0.00	0.00	0.00
ELECT. ROUGH	$6,650.00	$0.00	$6,650.00	0.00	6,650.00
ELECT.-FIXTURES	$1,560.00	$0.00	$1,560.00	0.00	1,560.00
H V A C	$8,750.00	$0.00	$8,750.00	0.00	8,750.00
BATH FAN	$400.00	$0.00	$400.00	0.00	400.00
SHEETMETAL	$1,250.00	$0.00	$1,250.00	0.00	1,250.00
ROOFING	$8,500.00	$0.00	$8,500.00	0.00	8,500.00
FIREPLACE	$0.00	$0.00	$0.00	0.00	0.00
WINDOWS / GLASS	$2,700.00	$0.00	$2,700.00	0.00	2,700.00
INSULATION	$1,125.00	$0.00	$1,125.00	0.00	1,125.00
DRYWALL / DRYWALL PATCH	$7,410.00	$0.00	$7,410.00	0.00	7,410.00

	Prelim Budget	Actual Budget	Variance	Change Orders	Total Budget
STUCCO / STUCCO PATCH	$3,250.00	$0.00	$3,250.00	0.00	3,250.00
CABINETS	$1,500.00	$0.00	$1,500.00	0.00	1,500.00
LUMBER FINISH	$850.00	$0.00	$850.00	0.00	850.00
CARPENTRY-FINISH LABOR	$1,550.00	$0.00	$1,550.00	0.00	1,550.00
RAILINGS	$0.00	$0.00	$0.00	0.00	0.00
STAIRS	$0.00	$0.00	$0.00	0.00	0.00
DOORS / JAMBS	$0.00	$0.00	$0.00	0.00	0.00
PAINTING INTERIOR	$8,500.00	$0.00	$8,500.00	0.00	8,500.00
PAINTING EXTERIOR	$2,200.00	$0.00	$2,200.00	0.00	2,200.00
GARAGE DOOR	$0.00	$0.00	$0.00	0.00	0.00
MASONRY / VENEER	$0.00	$0.00	$0.00	0.00	0.00
CERAMIC TILE SHOWERS	$2,225.00	$0.00	$2,225.00	0.00	2,225.00
CERAMIC TILE DECK	$0.00	$0.00	$0.00	0.00	0.00
CERAMIC TILE BACKSPLASH	$0.00	$0.00	$0.00	0.00	0.00
FORMICA TOPS	$0.00	$0.00	$0.00	0.00	0.00
GRANITE TOPS	$0.00	$0.00	$0.00	0.00	0.00
MARBLE TOPS	$0.00	$0.00	$0.00	0.00	0.00
QUARTZ TOPS	$7,580.00	$0.00	$7,580.00	0.00	7,580.00
WROUGHT IRON	$0.00	$0.00	$0.00	0.00	0.00
DECKING	$0.00	$0.00	$0.00	0.00	0.00
SHOWER PAN	$450.00	$0.00	$450.00	0.00	450.00
HARDWARE-FINISH	$0.00	$0.00	$0.00	0.00	0.00
CARPET	$0.00	$0.00	$0.00	0.00	0.00
VINYL FLOORING	$0.00	$0.00	$0.00	0.00	0.00
TILE FLOORING	$660.00	$0.00	$660.00	0.00	660.00
MARBLE FLOORING	$0.00	$0.00	$0.00	0.00	0.00
WOOD FLOORING / REFINISHING	$4,160.00	$0.00	$4,160.00	0.00	4,160.00
SKYLIGHTS / SOLATUBES	$0.00	$0.00	$0.00	0.00	0.00
SHOWER ENCL.	$1,450.00	$0.00	$1,450.00	0.00	1,450.00
MIRRORS	$0.00	$0.00	$0.00	0.00	0.00
WARDROBE DOORS	$0.00	$0.00	$0.00	0.00	0.00
APPLIANCES	$0.00	$0.00	$0.00	0.00	0.00
RANGE HOOD	$0.00	$0.00	$0.00	0.00	0.00
CLEAN UP	$3,500.00	$0.00	$3,500.00	0.00	3,500.00
WEATHERSTRIP	$0.00	$0.00	$0.00	0.00	0.00
ATTIC LADDER	$0.00	$0.00	$0.00	0.00	0.00
U.G. UTILITIES	$0.00	$0.00	$0.00	0.00	0.00
HOUSE LATERALS	$0.00	$0.00	$0.00	0.00	0.00
SEWER CONN.	$0.00	$0.00	$0.00	0.00	0.00
WATER SYSTEM	$0.00	$0.00	$0.00	0.00	0.00
SUB-DRAINS	$0.00	$0.00	$0.00	0.00	0.00
SOLAR PANELS	$0.00	$0.00	$0.00	0.00	0.00
PAVING	$0.00	$0.00	$0.00	0.00	0.00
INTERCOM SYS.	$0.00	$0.00	$0.00	0.00	0.00
FINE GRADING	$0.00	$0.00	$0.00	0.00	0.00
FLATWORK / WALKS	$0.00	$0.00	$0.00	0.00	0.00
LANDSCAPING	$0.00	$0.00	$0.00	0.00	0.00
FENCES / WALLS	$1,500.00	$0.00	$1,500.00	0.00	1,500.00
ROOF GUTTERS	$0.00	$0.00	$0.00	0.00	0.00
WALKTHRU PREP	$0.00	$0.00	$0.00	0.00	0.00

	Prelim Budget	Actual Budget	Variance	Change Orders	Total Budget
SANDBLASTING	$0.00	$0.00	$0.00	0.00	0.00
GENERAL LABOR	$1,000.00	$0.00	$1,000.00	0.00	1,000.00
INSURANCE	$2,355.00	$0.00	$2,355.00	0.00	2,355.00
SUPERINENDENT	$12,000.00	$0.00	$12,000.00	0.00	12,000.00
GENERAL ADMINSTRATIVE & OVERHEAD	$1,190.00	$0.00	$1,190.00	0.00	1,190.00
CONTINGENCY	$2,050.00	$0.00	$2,050.00	0.00	2,050.00
CONTRACTOR FEE	$12,000.00	$0.00	$12,000.00	0.00	12,000.00
TOTAL JOB COSTS	**$157,545.00**	$0.00	$157,545.00	0.00	$157,545.00

Client Feedback

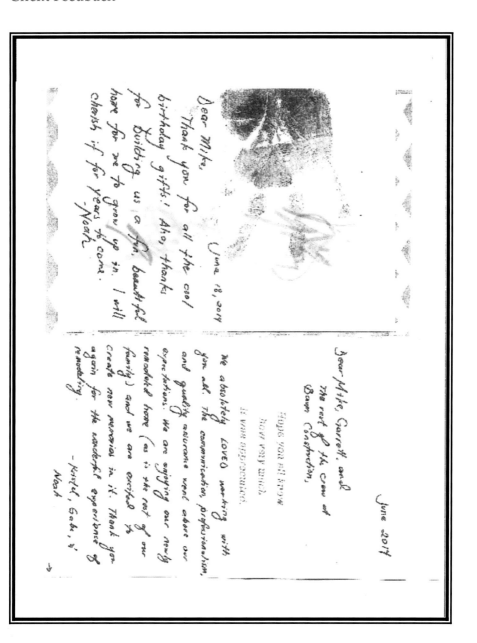

About the Author

Michael Baum with former CEO of General Electric Jack Welsh and business coach JT Foxx.

Michael Baum has been in the building and construction industry for over 40 years. He started in the homebuilding business as an apprentice union carpenter in 1972, completed a four-year apprenticeship in three years by going to summer school, thereby earning his journeyman certificate. Michael worked as a carpenter on residential housing tracts for several more years.

In 1977 was granted a general contractor's license in the state of California and began working as a general contractor on residential projects. Shortly thereafter he was recruited by a homebuilder to be an on-site superintendent on a housing tract. From 1979 through 1990 Michael served in the capacity as a field superintendent for some of the top homebuilders in Southern California.

Over the next 12 years Michael took on increasing positions of responsibility in the homebuilding industry, culminating in the position of Vice President of Construction for a national homebuilding company in their Los Angeles Division.

During Michael's career, he has been responsible for the construction of over $1 billion dollars of residential and commercial developments, to include over 4,000 homes and remodels.

From October 2002 to September 2007 Michael was a Sr. Managing Partner at Newport Sierra LLC., a small infill builder based in Downey. During that time Newport Sierra LLC built a number of rental projects for their own portfolio. During the real estate crash of 2007 financing for such projects became unavailable and they ceased construction operations.

In 2010 Michael opened Baum Construction and Development to the public, as a full-service general contracting and remodeling firm based in Long Beach California.

Michael Baum with speaker, real estate investor, trainer and coach Phill Grove.

During his career Michael also earned a Bachelor of Science and Master's Degree in Business Administration.

Michael has served on numerous boards for Construction Associations to include:

Advisory Board Construction Technology / Don Bosco Tech (2001-2004)
Board of Directors Residential Purchasing Corporation (2001-2011)
Board of Directors / Building Industry Association Los Angeles County East Chapter (2005-2009)
President / Building Industry Association Los Angeles East Chapter (2007-2008)
Board of Directors Remodelers Council Orange County (2013-present)
Vice President Remodelers Council of Orange County (2014)

Michael is the president and CEO of Baum Companies, Inc. and its subsidiaries:
Baum Construction & Development   *Baum Luxury Homes*
Baum Construction Management   *Pacific Property Investments LLC.*

Made in the USA
Middletown, DE
30 August 2020